Retirement:

GREAT IDEA!
SCARY MOVE!

D1736819

Retirement:

Great Idea!

Scary Move!

A Life Transition Workbook

Phyllis R. Weingarten ACSW LCSW

GREAT IDEA! SCARY MOVE! PRESS ™
New York • Florida

Dedicated to my grandchildren
AVA and BRETT
May they always follow their dreams.

And in honor of
GRANDMA MOSES
Grandma Moses turned out her first painting

when she was 76 years old.

During her lifetime she painted more

than 1,000 pictures, 25 of them after she had

passed her 100th birthday.

Contents

Acknowledgements

This project has been both a personal creative effort and labor of love, from its conception as a workshop to its current combination of a workshop and workbook.

I wish to thank the following people who have traveled this journey with me:

Blanche and Maurice Goldstein, who delighted in all my accomplishments big and small, a parenting style that continues to feed my independent spirit.

My husband Allan, whose cynical nature was kept in check while the years of writing and re-writing clicked away.

My son Jason, the "go-to guy" for any computer information or electronic glitches, of which there were many.

My daughter Leslie and son-in-law Robert offered great advice about design.

Kathi Elster was the first person I called on for direction in shaping my workshop: *When Everyday is Saturday*. Her patience, encouragement, and professional skills and guidance were also helpful in bringing my workbook to fruition.

My patient, helpful relatives and friends who agreed to read yet another revision of my workbook and help me to market my workshop or generally root me on.

Doris Lehman, Christine Robertello, Susan Jacobson, Debra Hirsch-Boyle, Marilyn Hirsch, Susan Herman, Andrea Granet, Linda and Rob Rosier, Barbara and Jerome Albenberg, Gaby Shanon, Bonnie Tarlowe, Stan Roban, Lorraine and Merrill Eastman all deserve mention and thanks.

I am very grateful to my editor Naomi Rosenblatt for her vision to expand and merge the workshop with the workbook. It was a fun and productive summer of 2012 that formed the essence of *Retirement: Great Idea! Scary Move!*.

Introduction

If you've picked up this book, you're ready to make changes. Whether you're contemplating a big transition like retirement, or you've already begun changing your life and want more insight into where you're going, you will find guidance in the following pages. This workbook focuses on issues that pertain to retirement, but the exercises and mentoring can be applied to any life transition.

The workbook is designed to accompany a four-week course offered by me, Phyllis R. Weingarten, ACSW LCSW. A retired social worker, I created the class because I found that my husband and I had only a financial retirement plan in place. While it was a good beginning, the financial plan left many other questions unaddressed as we headed into a retired lifestyle. The mystery caught me off guard and inspired this class and workbook. The exercises I'll share with you here grew from years of training and soul-searching. They reflect my life and those of my former students.

This workbook can be completed with or without the classroom structure. If you're working on your own, you may want to pace yourself along the four blocks of time that reflect the four class sessions. It may also be helpful to have support as you delve into the workbook, such as a small group of friends who are also doing the program.

Whether you're in a class, a small group or doing the program independently, you may hit a wall or two. And if you find yourself struggling, congratulate yourself: you're on the right road. True progress is not always steady, and you will work through the thorny patches and keep going.

At this point it must be noted that these exercises and self-reflections may raise strong emotions. You are encouraged to explore and express these emotions rather than sitting on them and allowing them to fester. The class puts you in touch with your feelings, but is not intended to replace psychotherapy or counseling. If you are inclined to explore your life in greater depth, I encourage you to seek out a psychotherapist, counselor, or life coach of your choice.

The book is divided into classroom and homework exercises. Some exercises entail short multiple-choice answers, while others involve extensive writing. You'll notice that I have provided sample answers or "prompts" for some of the more open-ended questions. Please don't feel you need to duplicate my sample answers. They are intended only as prompts, to further clarify the questions for you and to illustrate the kinds of answers that might come up. They are meant to stimulate your own thinking. As further help, I offer mentoring and share my own personal stories.

You will come away from this work with access to new tools of vision and a retirement "business plan." Your plan will include a Mission Statement and a Timeline for launching the necessary steps. You might also come away from this class with new friends, and new confidence in yourself. You will certainly come away with a living document, a journal of self-discovery that can help you navigate your future. Congratulations on your choice to embark upon this exciting journey!

Now, it's time for push off...

Part 1

A Different Way
of Seeing

"When we create something, we always create it first in a thought form. A thought or idea always precedes manifestation."

— SHAKTI GAWAIN, *Creative Visualization*

Class One: Retirement as Opportunity

Theme:

Our unique answers live inside us and we can learn to access them.

Beginning Tool of Vision:

Quick Reflection/Free Association "off-the-top-of-your head"

The Concept of Vision

Your success in the next phase of life will be based upon your ability to let go of what was or, perhaps even more challenging, to let go of what wasn't. And your success will depend equally upon your ability to use skills you've learned and to draw sustenance from relationships you've cultivated throughout your life. In other words, as you move forward you will release the past, and you will also make good use of the past.

You can open up to new possibilities for yourself as you become a person of vision. This workshop will provide you with different tools of vision to help you access the answers that are already inside of you. These answers will become keystones for planning this next phase in your life.

Vision, in the sense this workbook describes, is not merely the optical ability to see. Vision is the ability to see beyond our present reality, to create what does not yet exist, to become what we aren't … as yet. It gives us the opportunity to tap into our imagination instead of being bound by our memory, hopes, and fears.

What we know about Vision:

1. Ideas and insights might need time and coaxing, or might occur suddenly.

2. There is no right or wrong vision. There are only visions that feel right or wrong for you. You recognize visions that reflect you and what you want for your life because they hold your attention and excite you.

3. Visions have different forms, styles, and content. They may appear as a sentence or paragraph (heard within yourself, spoken by a friend, read in a book); an image that you see in a film, museum, or magazine, or a picture you imagine. Or they may appear as a mental concept to which you respond with emotion.

First Exercise: Your Current Vision of Retirement

Associate quickly, freely, and spontaneously for a set amount of time like 1 or 2 minutes. Use a timer, if need be. Write with your non-dominant hand if you wish. Do not edit. Do not censor. Trust your first sparks and flashes.

What associations does the word 'retirement' bring up for me?
List five words:

_____

_____

Why do I want to change my daily life?

_____

_____

What does 'conversation' mean to me?

_____

_____

What would I like to know about myself by the end of today's conversation?

_____

_____

After doing this exercise, share with others whatever you wish to reveal. This process of tuning in and sharing outwardly becomes the basis of all conversation, and all change.

The Difference between Having a Vision and Constructing a Vision

Imagination is the ability to form mental images and ideas, especially of events never seen or experienced directly. Imagination is the source of vision, such as the vision of having power and wealth, or the vision of being a writer — none of which necessarily represent the imaginer's current reality.

But this initial idea or image is the tool that we use to construct a vision. Identifying this idea may be called "having a vision." Constructing a vision, on the other hand, has broader purpose and includes more detail than the first flash. A constructed vision includes specific steps to help us actualize our initial vision.

The initial vision can be spontaneous as in an "aha/epiphany/light bulb" moment that just seems to come to you. The constructed vision requires some logic and precision, as though you were designing a puzzle and then testing it by putting the pieces together. These pieces will come from the facilitated exercises in this workbook, exercises intended to raise your awareness.

A constructed vision guides energy into concrete manifestation, whether it is long-term or short-term. Constructing a vision in this workshop means writing your business plan for a successful retirement, based on your initial visions invoked in these exercises. You will refer to this plan and you will modify it throughout your life, if and when necessary.

A Vision for Retirement, whether yours is an early retirement because you've been downsized from your job, or late because you love your work, can function as an opportunity to refine the dream of your life. A retiring person needs courage, perseverance, tenacity, and … the knowledge that she or he has permission to be happy and fulfilled at this special time.

Throughout your professional life, you've been busy achieving your goals. Time for reflection has been limited. You now have the opportunity to launch a retirement exactly the same way you would launch any new enterprise — on the shoulders of your previous experience and success, and by being open to helpful change.

To succeed, you'll want to use every tool you've mastered, every contact you've nurtured, and every experience you've weathered. You want to triumph, leave a legacy, maybe even make money, definitely have fun. But most of all, go after the dreams you've been dreaming since you were young.

Phyllis' Story: Starting the Conversation

One day, I had an epiphany about retirement. I realized that it was not just about money. I asked myself, "Is this all there is?" This discovery went against a lifetime of believing otherwise, because financial was the only plan I had when I retired.

What else did retirement mean? I needed to find out.

To help them find their way, people speak with therapists. As a therapist, I realized that I had to have some serious conversations with myself.

As a licensed clinical social worker with 25 years of professional experience, I've helped individuals, couples, and families cope effectively with life cycle transitions. My own life cycle transition — retirement — required self-help that I didn't expect.

Today I walk the walk as a retiree whose life was initially turned around by my husband's retirement from an international accounting firm. When my husband announced that he wanted to spend more time in Florida and play sports all day, it was the wake-up call to my own lack of planning.

Outdoor activities like tennis and golf were always central to his life, but somehow I didn't realize how very much he loved hot weather. His statement became worthy of my full attention when I realized how much I didn't like hot weather.

So I had to think fast and hard. I asked myself, "What do I like? What do I want? How can I find happiness alongside my husband who is pursuing happiness his way?"

My initial response was to commit myself to another year of work. (We are all entitled to brief stints of denial, avoidance, and detours at different junctures in our lives. *Brief* is the key word.)

The year passed quickly and it was time to act. I let go of my work structure. The world quickly declared me retired, whatever that was supposed to mean. Personally, my status felt a bit murkier.

The finality of this transition took my breath away. I wondered how I managed to find myself in this position without a plan. A therapist giving no thought to the non-financial aspects of retirement is like a shoemaker with frayed soles.

The Three Pillars

Asking myself what retirement required, I realized that there are three pillars of a fulfilling solution: financial security, physical health, and psychological planning. Just like a three-legged stool, if one support is missing the other two cannot stand. My psychological plan was missing.

My conversation led me to ask myself what I wanted to do with the rest of my life. I enjoyed my work as a therapist, and I saw no reason to give up this satisfying part of my life just because I was leaving my day-to-day practice. The answer was that I wanted to venture into the field of entrepreneurship, quite a risky turn for someone like me whose experience, and comfort zone, lay within bureaucratic structures. I saw that I would do what I knew how to do, but I would just do it differently. I also wanted a flexible work schedule with content that was transportable. In that way I could support a lifestyle of increased leisure and traveling.

My retirement journey began as I applied the professional skills, knowledge, and experience that I'd practiced, as a clinical social worker, to help myself. I had to focus on and challenge the automatic pilot in my life, an exercise both exhilarating and quite scary. My tolerance for change was about to be tested, big time. Intuitively, I understood that *familiar* is comforting, yet *new* is important. Unprepared, I had no choice but to travel this new road.

I discovered that knowing how I felt about the changes that retirement brings is critical to success. While moving forward, I learned to recognize my strengths and move past obstacles like anxiety and procrastination. My new way of working represented the balance that I craved in my life for work, play, and creativity. I kept the familiar, that is, what I knew how to do. Then I incorporated the new, which evolved as workshops in which I shared my discovery.

From my personal and professional experience, I now know that the retirement conversation is about re-creation and the journey is about pursuing dreams. My journey led me to find a way to put my conversations, plans, visions, and goals into a workbook I want to share with you.

Second Exercise: Assess Your Tolerance for Unexpected Change

There are two kinds of changes in our lives: those we choose, and those we do not choose and often don't expect. The exercise below pertains to unexpected change.

Remember a time when change knocked at your door unexpectedly. Describe it in two sentences, such as: *My spouse asked for a divorce. I was offered a job overseas. I learned I was pregnant. I got fired. I was diagnosed as pre-diabetic.*

Write your experience:

How did you feel at the time? What actions did you take?

Looking back, do you feel this change presented an opportunity?
How do you perceive it now?

Describe your typical response to unexpected change.
How do you tend to handle it?
Do you resist it or welcome it? Are you passive or proactive?
Do you perceive opportunities or burdens ... or a bit of both?

Third Exercise: Assess Your Tolerance for Initiating Change and Taking Risks

As we travel through life from childhood into adulthood we develop habits. As we go on, we often create rituals to support certain habits. Over time, these habits and supportive rituals become our personalized comfort zone.

Most times these habits, and the rituals that support them, serve us well. Other times, not so much. This next exercise will help you become aware of the difference between those habits and rituals that serve you well, and others that interfere with the positive flow in your life.

For example, Max was a straight 'A' student and liked it that way. His habit and ritual of not socializing during his allotted study time served a constructive purpose; he did not waiver and he planned accordingly.

Emily's habit to feel in control of her leisure activities ultimately gave her the reputation amongst her friends as a "switch hitter." She ritualistically changed the date and time of any social plan, feigning a last-minute conflict. Emily's friends, believing that a last minute "better "offer arose, became reluctant to make dates with her. Emily was not able to see past her need to feel "in control," nor to understand that this pattern of behavior was interfering with her social relationships.

Punctuality was Evan's forte. He was not able to divert from being "on time," no matter the psychological cost to himself or others. It would not occur to him to communicate about a sudden change or to apologize for extenuating circumstances. He felt he had to be perfect.

As we plan our futures we must bear in mind how rarely we challenge our life scripts. Remaining in our comfort zones is understandable because change can be unsettling. A human response to change can range from feeling anxious, resentful, and upset to being utterly clueless. However, we journey into the future with power as we become able to make helpful changes. Otherwise, we may become bound by old habits and stumble over our status quo.

This workbook will help you to identify and ultimately remove yourself from the automatic pilot in your life so that you may balance your basic need for continuity with a healthy openness to change.

The following exercise introduces a scale of attitudes toward making changes. Answer these questions on the basis of how you feel now. Take about two minutes to complete all the questions.

High means "Yes. Bring it on!"
Medium means "Now and then."
Low means "No. Don't rock the boat!"

Psychological Change: Change in outlook, skills, and attitude

I am intrigued by different viewpoints:

Low   Medium Low   Medium   Medium High   High

I like learning new skills:

Low   Medium Low   Medium   Medium High   High

On the job, I prefer to "wear different hats" and multi-task:

Low   Medium Low   Medium   Medium High   High

I read a wide variety of books:

Low   Medium Low   Medium   Medium High   High

I enjoy finding new ways to solve problems:

Low   Medium Low   Medium   Medium High   High

General Score for Psychological Change:

Low   Medium Low   Medium   Medium High   High

Physical Change: Change of environment and appearance

I like moving to different homes:

Low   Medium Low   Medium   Medium High   High

I often rearrange furniture and change the look of my home:

Low   Medium Low   Medium   Medium High   High

I enjoy travel:

Low   Medium Low   Medium   Medium High   High

I experiment with different hairstyles and (for men) beard or mustache styles:

Low   Medium Low   Medium   Medium High   High

I often cancel plans, or suggest plans on the spur of the moment:

Low   Medium Low   Medium   Medium High   High

General Score for Physical Change:

Low   Medium Low   Medium   Medium High   High

General Tolerance for Initiating Changes and Taking Risks

Circle the sentence that best describes you:

"I love the thrill of variety and adventure. I often introduce big changes into my life that are not even necessary. Change keeps me alive."

"I enjoy the challenge and stimulation of change, and easily integrate new plans into my established routines."

"I seek change only after I've had the chance to reflect and research my options. I need a strong motivation to change, but adapt reasonably well to the new circumstances I've chosen."

"I make small, selective changes if they're absolutely necessary. I don't enjoy making changes, and I don't over-do it."

"I strive to keep things as they are, because I've made them this way for a reason. I value stability and prefer to avoid change and disruption."

Look over all your answers on pages 20-22. Which of the five options did you circle most frequently? Which of the last five sentences most called out to you? With this in mind, rate your overall tolerance for initiating change and taking risks:

Low   Medium Low   Medium   Medium High   High

Briefly summarize your tolerance for changing and taking risks.
What have you learned about yourself and your comfort zone as you answered these questions?

Phyllis's Story: My Own Tolerance for Change

The words of two friends, delivered at different junctures in my life, are examples of my response to the opportunity for change knocking at my door.

One friend, who was also a colleague, suggested that in order to establish a successful private practice I quit my full-time job. She believed that would enable me to focus my time and energy and thus be able to achieve my goals. I claimed that it was easy for her to say since she had been forced to create a structure (a private practice) and had not let go of her job.

My friend believed that my feelings of sheer terror would create the drive and motivation for me to succeed, independent of an existing work structure. With the best intentions, she was wrong. I had practically no comfort level with change, and a great need for structure.

A few years later another friend, with a demonstrated entrepreneurial spirit, closed a family business. He told me that by leaving my job and its existing work structure, I would walk down the street and "see" life differently. He perceived this experience as opportunity.

I claimed that it was easy for him to say, and listed a catalog of reasons why it was simpler for him than for me to leave a familiar structure.

Again, my initial emotional response was sheer terror. However, this time my emotions were sprinkled with exhilaration. The potential to "see" life differently and acquire the freedom to do what I wanted to do, when I wanted to do it was compelling. Now my feelings were a mixture of fear and excitement.

Still, I stored away his advice and gave some excuse about the value of my current job as a way of rationalizing my need to maintain the status quo. That, in turn, was the rather limited range of my comfort zone for change. Ultimately, to no one's surprise, I burned out. At last, I felt that I had no choice but to leave my safe structure. And that is where my retirement story began.

Hindsight 101: Could Have, Would Have, Should Have

A well-structured re-visit to the past can be a useful exercise to open you up to new possibilities by recognizing the consequences of your tolerance for change. Do these exercises quickly and write the first response that comes into your mind.

Do not hang out in the past too long.

I wish I had

_____

_____

I was too scared to

_____

_____

My major disappointment is

_____

_____

I feel lucky to have

_____

_____

I had the courage to

_____

_____

My major accomplishment is

_____

_____

Weigh the ups and downs, highs and lows. Take two minutes to describe how your scale of past experience is currently tipped:

_____

_____

_____

_____

_____

_____

Fourth Exercise: Take a Bus Tour of Yourself

With the relaxed eye of a sightseer, describe who have you been and where are you going. What might a tour guide say about you?

Here are some quick questions to prompt you:

Think of three things you do each day.

What do you do on special days?

Where would you most want to be on a warm, sunny day?

What do you worry about and why?

What are your three greatest burdens?

What are three favorite parts of your life?

How would you describe yourself physically?

How would you describe yourself socially?

Compose a short, honest, and lighthearted paragraph of how a tour guide might describe you today. Have some fun. Include key details, such as physical description, habits, skills, and personality traits. You can write a paragraph from scratch, or base it on our template from a tour book that you'll find on the next page.

BUS TOUR OF _____

Visiting _____ can be intensely _____ .

_____ 's _____ energy has been known to

keep people _____ . With _____ and _____ ,

_____ can _____ .

Generally _____ and _____ , _____ ,

has been a _____ _____ and _____ ,

and an _____ .

Sample Bus Tour of "Wendy"

Visiting **Wendy** can be intensely **inspiring. Wendy's compassionate** energy has been known to keep people **focused.** With **kindness** and **sparkle, Wendy** can **clarify the challenges.** Generally **warm** and **insightful, Wendy** has been a **popular counselor and therapist,** and an **unforgettable friend, mother, grandmother, and wife.**

If you prefer, use this space to write your own tour guide description:

_____

_____

_____

_____

Was it easy or difficult for you to take this tour? What came up for you?

If you wish, paste a photograph of yourself here:

Homework Assignments:

1. Make a Date with Yourself

Inspiration can come from a variety of places. The site may depend on your mood or the availability of privacy. Be flexible. Experiment with different locations. This is your journey of discovery so be open to possibilities. For example, you can:

View the horizon from a beach. You might be alone or among a crowd. The expanse of the ocean, whether from under an umbrella or a walk on the sand, can help to open your mind.

Walk in the woods. Ambling along may offer you serenity and the solitary mental nourishment you need. The variety of sights and sense of adventure might inspire you.

Stroll through a park. You can be social or alone, whether sitting on a bench or admiring the trees and flowers. Either stillness or motion — or both — can aid in tapping into your mind.

Visit a museum. This can be a solitary, stimulating experience. Art can provoke, excite, disturb, or overwhelm. There are many choices, for instance, you might contemplate one work of art or meditate in an outdoor sculpture garden.

Go to a spa. These getaways are places to feel nurtured. If touch is therapeutic for you, the luxury of being pampered may open your mind.

Withdraw into your garden. If you're lucky enough to have one, you can putter, think, or feel, or do all at once. Your garden is your creation, so in it you may feel open to new possibilities for your future.

Journeys aren't limited to places outside your home. When you are alone, explore. For some people, a lingering bath, along with scented candles, is the perfect place to relax and let their minds wander. For others, a favorite chair, a view from a window, or a cherished sight from a porch can provide an ideal setting for the inner journey.

Give yourself the gift of time. Relax. Concentrate. Remember that it is your journey. Think only of yourself.

Some of my favorite spots for contemplation include:

A chaise at home that acts as my cocoon, providing a safe place for thoughts and feelings.

The beach, with its expansive "anything is possible feeling" that comes from viewing the horizon of water and open space.

The diverse neighborhoods of New York City, which feed my spirit, energy, and total feeling of well-being when I wander through them.

During one of my reveries, the title of the musical "Stop the World, I Want To Get Off" popped into my head. It was a fitting metaphorical description for my life.

What I uncovered was that I had all too well internalized the dictates of family and society. Change was needed to synchronize what was inside and what was outside. A process that I call "Peeling the Artichoke" began to show me the best of what was inside. I call it that because "Peeling the Artichoke" describes the paradoxical process of letting go of who you are in order to become who you are destined to be. You must peel away some layers because when you do, the most satisfying part will be revealed.

So, I took a look at my life — taking a trip with new eyes — on the same journey that I now take you.

2. Take a 'Bus Tour' of Your Home with the same relaxed tourist's eye that enabled you to take a tour of yourself. Jot down your impressions, as though they came from a tour guide. Be prepared to share them in the next session.

This tourist's view will give you a fresh picture of how your environment reveals your life. You will be surprised at what you discover. Remember to keep notes on your observations. All of them can be used in your ultimate plan.

Below are some prompts:

Walk from room to room. Observe carefully the colors, textures, and design. What do you see? What feelings and thoughts come to mind?

Go into a favorite room. Why is it special?

_____

_____

Go into your least favorite room. Why do you feel this way about it?

_____

_____

Take mental pictures, just as you do when you visit a new place. What do you know about the person living here?

_____

_____

_____

_____

Samples of What Do You Know About the Person Who Lives Here?

He loves ships and sailing. There are many paintings of seascapes, and of yachts and schooners. The walls are either pale blue or white. You may also say that this resident 'runs a tight ship' because every room is so tidy and clean. The bedroom is especially peaceful. There's no television, but a ship in a bottle and collection of seashells on the dresser.

This home is a junk pile! You can hardly walk without colliding head-on with this person's past. Boxes of old books and clothing, broken musical instruments, and outmoded answering machines are everywhere. This person must find it hard to make decisions about what to keep from the past and what to let go.

Was it easy or difficult for you to take this tour? What came up for you?

_____

_____

_____

_____

_____

If you wish, paste a photograph of your favorite room here:

"Imagine that you are asked to choose what you like about yourself and your life and to pack all of those things into a suitcase to take with you in the next century. What will you put into storage? How much space will you leave open for your future?"

— JAMES E. BIRREN AND LINDA FELDMAN,

Where to Go From Here?

Class Two: Keepers and Changers

Theme:

Our unique desires about what we wish to keep in our lives, and what we wish to change, live inside us. They show us not only what we *don't* want, but also what we want. We can learn to access these desires with tools of vision.

Beginning Tool of Vision:

Expanded Reflection: Articulating the details of a new possible life. Quick, instinctive thoughts rise to the next level through reflection and writing.

Vision Creates Consequence

The kind of vision you embrace has significant consequences:

Practical vision will lead you to make choices based on what is obvious and simple. For example, you may decide to "stay put" rather than leave your home of 25 years — even though you're tired of it and would prefer to live in a warmer climate. It's less complicated than pulling up stakes. Or you may wish to live near your family, even though you don't like that region yourself. This kind of choice is right for some people but not for all.

Illusory vision is based on hopes and fancies. Don't count on it to produce the expected results. For instance, when you imagine that changing aspects of your life, like your geographical location or your partner will make you happy, you are likely to be disappointed. Change starts inside, not outside.

Social vision reflects the expectations of others. For example, friends are buying homes in Florida. Staying with the pack is crucial for your self-esteem, so you buy a home in Florida even though you dislike the tropics. You do not want to be left out. If you use their reflection to shape your choices you will not be following your own custom-designed life script.

Power vision is connected specifically to you. This vision reflects your preferences, dreams, and wishes. But it's also plausible and easy to implement in well-considered steps. Power vision honors your dreams and makes sense for your life.

Here's an example of how a person really came to understand how vision creates consequence. Joe's vision of owning a small company had seemed like a fantasy or illusory vision at first. But, he was able to add a practical aspect that transformed it into his power vision:

Retired from a senior sales position with a multinational corporation, Joe had no specific plans other than desiring more flexibility in his life. He did, however, identify a dream of being in charge of a small company. He'd always worked for others, and felt that his ability to lead and manage a sales team could be applied even more.

A few months later, Joe started to receive calls from his international former clients. They complained that orders were not being filled, phone calls to the corporation were not returned, and, therefore, delivery schedules were seriously disrupted.

Could he solve this problem? He tried, but when his phone calls to the corporate leadership were not returned, Joe began to visualize a business opportunity. His fleeting fantasies over the years of owning a business re-emerged. Now his fortune would be directly linked to his vision, ability, and experience.

Joe surveyed his former customers in order to establish the profitability for this market; even a past competitor was interested in having Joe represent her product, in a freelance capacity. Going forward, he would assume more responsibility and enjoy the flexibility of managing his own accounts. He could do it all without corporate bureaucracy.

Joe would do what he knew how to do, but he would do it differently. He wrote a plan that combined a new venture, along with his retirement wish list. This was a perfect match for a person seeking a sense of purpose, together with a love of travel and a desire to enjoy more leisure time with his family, particularly his grandchildren.

His accomplishment is a great example of blending an entrepreneurial spirit with specific interests and experience. Joe was using his business skills and experience (familiar) to launch his own company (new).

Joe's initiative and success is a perfect example of a creative retirement. The combination of his choices resulted in the right balance, for him, of what is familiar with the pre-requisite change to meet the needs of a different lifestyle.

First Exercise: Role Models as a Point of Vision

Role models, whether positive or negative, are powerful influences in our lives. They can be our parents, siblings, a member of our extended family, colleagues, friends, teachers, mentors, or a famous person (dead or alive) with whom we have no personal relationship.

We can start by looking at the example set by our parents' retirements:

1. Did one or both of your parents retire?

2. If they retired, was it voluntary or involuntary?

3. If they retired, did your parents discuss or plan for retirement?

4. If they never retired, can you recall their thoughts and feelings about remaining at work as they got older?

Expanded reflection: Take 5-10 minutes to write about how your parents' example had influenced the choices you are now making for yourself. How do you see yourself as similar to, or as different from, your parents?

_____

_____

_____

_____

_____

Sample Reflection About Parents:

My parents were both employed until the day they announced that they were retiring and moving to Florida. They discussed and planned only with each other. My mother took a part-time administrative job in her Florida community while my father played golf and indulged in his love of ceramics.

My parent's finances were limited, so they visited us only once a year and we tried to visit them once a year. I vowed never to make an arbitrary decision to leave my children and grandchildren as my parents left my family and me. I have also spent much time "thinking" about retirement and lifestyle options. I know that having a conversation and planning is essential for my well-being and that of my children and grandchildren.

Power Role Models

How positive and inspiring are your parents and other role models? Would you describe any of them as Power Role Models — those that have strongly inspired you to follow your dreams?

Exercise: Take 5-10 minutes to describe four different Power Role Models and how they have inspired you:

NAME: INSPIRES ME TO:

Create the Space for Your Vision to Come True

It's important to deal with clutter. Living with excess may distract you and interfere with your ability to form a vision of what is, and what will be. Removing physical and mental clutter will give you a sense of being more grounded in the present and, of course, able to form the vision for your future.

Whether you enjoy or dislike clutter, it enables you to hold on to the past. A reflection of your anxiety about the future, clutter can be identified because it has little to do with your present life. The following exercises will expand your understanding about how each aspect of clutter — mental and physical — affects you.

Once clutter is removed, the challenge is to resist acting on the urge to "fill" the space. Open space, both physically and abstractly, symbolizes an opportunity to live in the present and tolerate the tension of leaving space for what can be, and what will be, in your future.

Second Exercise: Mental clutter

We'll look first at mental clutter. Here is my chart of typical items that clutter our minds and outlook. They can often be recognized by sentences you hear yourself saying over and over. I've provided my words. Take 5 minutes to fill in your own. Do not worry if sometimes your expressions coincide with mine:

MENTAL CLUTTER	THE WORDS I USED
Need for approval	"Do you like it?"
Procrastination	"I'm already overwhelmed."
Lack of discipline	"I can't find the time."
Lack of enthusiasm	"I have no clue."
Fear of failure	"I have to practice more."
Fear of success	"If this works, can I do it again?"
Fear of the unknown	"I can't do that."
Fear of pursuing dreams	"That's not reality."
Fear of living dreams	"Pipe dreams."
Debt	"Do you take American Express?"

MENTAL CLUTTER   THE WORDS YOU USE

Need for approval

Procrastination

Lack of discipline

Lack of enthusiasm

Fear of failure

Fear of success

Fear of the unknown

Fear of pursuing dreams

Fear of living dreams

Debt

Mental clutter can appear as the endless to-do list, never having the right tools, not feeling able to do something perfectly, morning fatigue, etc. These next questions will help you identify your mental clutter and describe how it impacts your life:

List four examples of your own mental clutter, such as worry, procrastination, grudges, insecurity, perfectionism, and so forth:

1. _____

2. _____

3. _____

4. _____

A Longer Reflection on the Impact of Mental Clutter

Choose one item from your list of mental clutter. Take 5-10 minutes to describe how you understand its presence in your life. Then describe what you have done — or will do — to modify this presence. (*For a sample prompt, please turn the page.*)

Two samples of the Mental Clutter Reflection:

My Need for Approval

I lived in the shadow of my older brother, whose life as an athlete, student, and leader at school flowed with ease and purpose. My parents treated him as the "could do no wrong kid." I seemingly starved for the limelight, acted accordingly and became the "could do no right" kid.

My competitive spirit served me well in athletics and academics but not in my relationship with my brother, and ultimately, with his wife. My competitiveness diverted positive energy into places that disrupted emotional connection.

One day I decided to come clean and apologize for my "competitive" need for attention and one-upmanship. I took responsibility for the strategies I used over the years, whether it was grabbing my parent's attention, boasting of my husband's raises and our material possessions or of one of my children's "successes." Surprisingly, my apology was accepted. We have been slowly building trust and a closer connection in our relationship and in those of our children.

Festering Anger

I was fired from a job for a completely bizarre reason that did not ring true. Meanwhile, they had delayed my paycheck for two months. I had good reason to be angry.

Eventually I was paid, but I remained sulky and bitter. I woke up in a glum mood. I felt helpless. Day in and day out, I re-lived the abuse I weathered from my boss and co-workers.

At some point, I realized that I had begun to enjoy this anger, because I knew so clearly that I was right. Little by little I focused less on those negative memories, and more on what I wanted to create.

Sometimes we clear away mental clutter quickly, and other times we need more time to do so. The process of recognizing and clearing away mental clutter will continue throughout our lives. Phyllis' story, on the facing page, illustrates how she overcame "thinking paralysis" over time.

Phyllis' Story about Procrastination

The Popular Duo: Perfectionism and Procrastination

For me, perfectionism, a lifetime foe, often led me into "thinking paralysis." As my friend and colleague Christine tells me, quite simply, that I think too much! Not surprisingly, Christine is a doer. My procrastination fed on a healthy diet of uncertainty and vacillation.

One of my goals for the past 10 years has been to expand the satisfying work of guiding people through the unfolding process of discovering their strengths, moving past the obstacles of procrastination and perfectionism, and enabling dreams to come true.

My process began by speaking with business people I knew about how to launch my own endeavor, and with publishing professionals about how to create a book. I asked questions and listened to answers. I also participated in workshops at the New School for Social Research and the Open Center in Manhattan. These events helped me believe in my dream of becoming an entrepreneur.

Once the idea for a workshop was hatched, I started to document my psychological journey with a journal as I traveled the retirement road.

I learned to quell my anxieties and become more of a doer by putting my work out into the world. I did so through marketing and presentations, and I became more confident as people registered for and attended my workshops.

The idea for the workbook emerged while speaking with a published author. In her opinion, the contents of my workshop had the potential to become a book. Her idea — reaching for something I hadn't considered — was bigger than I could have imagined.

Heeding my own advice about open-mindedness as preparation, I began work on my new project — converting my workshop material into a workbook format. Then, of course, I kept editing this workbook, worried that the final result wouldn't be "perfect," and about how it would be received.

"Just doing it" was a scary, but refreshing, breakthrough for me. I discovered that perfectionism can be valuable, too — but only if it is balanced with action. Otherwise, it is a one-way road to "thinking paralysis."

Third Exercise: Physical Clutter

Mental Clutter can be elusive because we can't see or touch it.

Physical clutter stares us in the face every day. Still, it can be difficult to identify this clutter because we grow accustomed to it, or we assign it some value. Physical clutter can appear in your spare room, the kitchen, the office, etc. List the four places in your home where your clutter gathers most, such as the garage, the chair in the dining room, your desk, the closet behind your desk:

1. _____

2. _____

3. _____

4. _____

List four unsolicited items that have found their way into your home, such as a neighbor's umbrella, the cracked vase your mother wanted you to repair, the ugly table from Aunt May, a friend's box of old sweaters:

1. _____

2. _____

3. _____

4. _____

List four objects that no longer give you pleasure or help you in any way, such as years of receipts that are kept for tax write-offs, kitchen utensils that have been replaced, the moldy ping-pong table in the basement, the broken sewing machine:

1. _____

2. _____

3. _____

4. _____

Take the time to look over each exercise. Ask yourself why you listed these items as your example of clutter. Write your feelings and associations with your physical clutter.

_____

_____

_____

_____

Choose an area or an item to de-clutter that is realistically possible for you to achieve. For example, a desktop drawer, a countertop, a closet, a tool shed, a hobby center, a study. Paste a before and an after picture in the space below. How do you feel about the change?

BEFORE   AFTER

Fourth Exercise: Finding the "Keepers" and "Changers" in your life

Identifying Keepers and Changers is the heart of this workbook.

During this session and the last, you've taken stock of yourself: You've assessed your tolerance for change, reviewed your ups and downs in hindsight, taken a bus tour of your home and yourself, identified role models, and explored mental and physical clutter in your life.

Now you'll take this self-inventory one step further and become specific about what you'd like to keep about your present life, and what you'd like to change. Complete the following fast exercises to determine what you value most in your life now. What you find will be called Keepers. Remember to take the time to clearly name each one.

If you need a jumpstart, consider the items on this list:

I feel the most joy and satisfaction when ...

- I get up in the morning and decide my daily activity
- Unstructured time is at a premium
- My daily planner is filled for a month at a glance
- I feel productive
- Time moves quickly and I'm not sure where the day went
- I feel a sense of purpose
- An opening exists in my schedule for a moment of solitude
- I feel the camaraderie of colleagues
- I am with my family and close friends
- I entertain and cook
- I walk around my home
- I absorb the culture in my community
- I put in a full day at the office

KEEPERS

These questions will help you to discover more details about your Keepers.

My four favorite jobs and what I liked about each:

1. _____

_____

2. _____

_____

3. _____

_____

4. _____

_____

The four most valuable skills I learned from my work place are:

1. _____

_____

2. _____

_____

3. _____

_____

4. _____

_____

My four favorite things to do at home:

1. _____

2. _____

3. _____

4. _____

My four outstanding gifts and talents:

1. _____

2. _____

3. _____

4. _____

My life gives me the most joy and satisfaction when I:

1. _____

_____

2. _____

_____

3. _____

_____

4. _____

_____

I celebrate life by:

1. _____

_____

2. _____

_____

3. _____

_____

4. _____

_____

Look over the answers that you've just written and think of what you've learned over the course of the exercises you've already done. Now list the 4 most important Keepers in your life:

1. _____

_____

2. _____

_____

3. _____

_____

4. _____

_____

Two sample Keepers lists:

1. A good marriage 2. Yearly travel with my wife   3. Playing golf
4. Involvement with our community

1. An active life-style 2. Living in New York City 3. Pursuing photography
4. A close relationship with my daughters and grandson

Tell Your Story

Take 5-10 minutes to describe your Keepers. Please feel free to elaborate on what you already knew and what you learned about yourself through these exercises. (*For a sample prompt, turn to page 50.*)

_____

_____

Two sample Keepers paragraphs:

I've been married to Regina for 40 years, and we've weathered a lot together and have become very close. Two years back we started traveling to a new place each year for about 10 days, and this has been a thrilling adventure. I also love playing golf and have made many friends doing so. Travel to a new place for 10 days a year and regular golf will keep me active and agile. I also value our community, and have enjoyed managing two local fundraisers. As a retired executive director of a non-profit, I can contribute my skills to help raise money for programs.

Keeping on-the-go has helped me stay strong and fit. I especially love walking in New York city, and swimming 3 times a week at the Y. I've been a photographer for 30 years, and now that I'm no longer photographing for catalogs and advertisements, I wish to explore nature photography. I can do that in Central Park, Riverside Park, the Catskills, and the Berkshires with my camera club. I love New York not only for its museums, galleries, and theatre, but because my daughters and grandson live here too. I see them all at least twice a month, and we do something fun together like eating dinner or seeing a Broadway show. If my daughter needs me to look after my grandson, I am happy to go cross-town and lend a hand. This way, I get to know him independently of her.

CHANGERS

Now, let's explore what you wish to change about your life, or your Changers. Where do you find the most dissatisfaction and frustration? Complete the following fast exercises to determine what frustrates you most in your life now. These results will be called Changers. Remember to take the time to clearly name each one.

If you need a jumpstart, consider the items on this list:

I feel 'my style is cramped' when ...

- I get up in the morning and must rush somewhere
  (or: I have nothing to do)
- My time is filled with obligations (or: I have nowhere to go)
- My daily planner is filled for a month at a glance (or: there are no plans)
- I feel stagnant and unproductive
- Time moves too quickly or too slowly and I'm not sure where the day went
- I feel no sense of purpose
- I have no time to breathe
- I mistrust my colleagues
- I am with my family (or I am not with my family)
- I entertain and cook (or I don't entertain and cook)
- I walk around my home
- I feel disconnected to my community
- I put in a full day at the office (or I do not go to work)

These questions will help you to discover more details about your Changers.

My four most difficult jobs and what I disliked about each:

1.

2.

3.

4.

My four greatest challenges and shortcomings:

1.

2.

3.

4.

My four least favorite things to do at home:

1. _____

2. _____

3. _____

4. _____

My four biggest regrets:

1. _____

2. _____

3. _____

4. _____

I find myself wanting more:

_____

_____

Look over the answers that you've just written and think of what you've learned over the course of the exercises you've already done. Now list the 4 most important Changers in your life:

1. _____

2. _____

3. _____

4. _____

Two sample Changers lists:

1. A troubled marriage 2. Too much money invested, not enough to enjoy now
3. Painful arthritis   4. Living in the same old place

1. A sedentary life-style   2. Small apartment   3. No creative outlet
4. Distant relationship with my son

Tell Your Story

Take 5-10 minutes to describe your Changers. Please feel free to elaborate on what you already knew and what you learned about yourself through these exercises. (*For a sample prompt, turn to page 56.*)

_____

_____

Two sample Changers paragraphs:

Ray and I have unfortunately grown apart. It may be time to let go, and become open to meeting other people while we're still young enough to do so. We have plenty of money, and I resent that he wants to keep so much of it invested in a volatile stock market while we skimp on travel or on continuing education. I don't want to be wasteful, but I do want to spend money while I have the mobility to enjoy it. I believe I can heal my stiff joints and arthritic pain through acupuncture, and I would love to live somewhere warmer and quieter than Chicago. We've lived here for decades, and I want to be near birds and flowers.

I find myself sitting around, watching TV, and playing chess all day. I've become practically immobile and have gained a lot of weight. I'm tired of my cramped city apartment. I could find a larger place for less money if I left New York and lived in Georgia near my family. I used to play bass, and wish I could be part of a jazz band again. I've completely lost touch with my son, my only child. I would like us to communicate more now.

TIP Using the lens of "Keepers and Changers" will help you discover what you love and how to adapt it creatively into your future. Below are some examples of how this might happen:

- Love of travel & food (Keeper) — become the food critic for your local community newspaper (Changer)
- Love to be in your boat on the water (Keeper) — get your captain's license and go into the tour business (Changer)
- Love of golf, tennis, basketball or other sport of your passion (Keeper) — mentor a child from the local boys or girls club, teach them the skills and values of this sport (Changer).
- A love of advocacy as practiced professionally (Keeper) — write a workbook that helps others to start the conversation that identifies the keepers and changers in their lives (Changer).

Keepers and Changers will inform your Vision of retirement.

Fifth Exercise: Initial Vision of Retirement

You will launch your retirement as you launch any other important endeavor — with a clearly structured and inspirational plan.

Your "business plan" will be a streamlined take-away from this class, and a living document of your personal roadmap for your new life. Today you'll take the first steps of imagining yourself as entrepreneurs and imagining your life as a start-up company you're creating.

Most business plans start with a Company Profile. Drawing from your tour highlights and your list of Keepers and Changers, begin to write the Company Profile for your 'retirement business plan.'

Answer the following questions:

1. What is your "company name?"

_____

(Prompts: Cora in Florida; Maria's New Lease on Life; A Frugal Feast; Writing My Novel; Old Home With New Colors; Time at Last to Sail; Tripping the Life Fantastic)

2. What is your guiding theme?

_____

_____

(Prompts: Moving to Florida permanently and painting; Divorcing Ray and going it alone with moxie; Getting the most bang from my limited bucks; Making the time to study, read, and write fiction; Transforming our home to be cheerful and livable enough for guests and parties; Prioritizing long yacht trips; Enjoying New York with my friends and family.)

3. Who is your success team?

_____

_____

_____

_____

(Prompts: My boyfriend, friends, stock broker, collectors, and art dealer; My friends, new and old; My friends and financial advisor; my book club, writing group, literary agent, and my son; My husband and our neighbors; My wife, our friends, and the crew; My friends, daughters, grandson, and camera club)

Now that you have given your business plan its own identity (name) and structure (theme), you can move forward with the critical work of outlining the essential steps that will guide you to realize the Keepers and Changers that will inform your Initial Vision of Retirement.

Homework Assignments

1. Go on a Date with Yourself, as you did last week. Maybe try a new location. When you get to your special place, write down the first Keeper you listed today on page 48:

_____

Write three exact steps you will take in order to sustain the Keeper. Think carefully and be precise.

1. _____

2. _____

3. _____

Then describe, in a quick, associative reflection, your emotions about taking these steps.

_____

_____

_____

_____

Next, write down the first Changer you listed today on page 54:

_____

Write three exact steps you will undergo in order to make the change real. Think carefully and be precise.

1. _____
_____

2. _____
_____

3. _____
_____

Then describe, in a quick, associative reflection, your emotions about taking these steps.

_____
_____
_____
_____
_____
_____

2. Meditation on Your Sense of Purpose

You may include this out on your date with yourself, or do it another time.

Put down your pen or pencil.

Close your eyes and take three deep breaths.

Begin to meditate on these three questions about your sense of purpose:

What do others say most often about you?

Which parts of your life bring you the greatest joy?

What do you feel you were put on earth to do?

Pick up your pen or pencil again and write the answers that came to you about your sense of purpose.

3. Do One Thing Differently This Week. Doing one thing differently can be life-changing. The change can be simple or profound.

- Choose something in your life to change — the way you see it or the way you do it — that will be different for you. In other words, modify a habitual behavior. For example, you might alter your route to the grocery store, re-arrange a room, reconnect with a long-lost relative, serve dinner with wine and candlelight, get a massage, resolve not to judge someone as he or she speaks, find a source for news other than your favorite TV channel.
- Once you've made your choice, write it down. Writing is a powerful tool for change.
- Practice your new behavior each day for a week.

Be aware of how well you are tolerating your choice to change. What are you feeling? Perhaps it is a sensation of flow as you move smoothly along the winding road of change. Or maybe you perceive feelings of resistance that require more effort as you push along with seemingly added mental or physical weight.

Write a description of how this small change affected your life:

Part 2

A Different Way
of Being

"Saying 'yes' to more things than we can actually manage to be present for with integrity and ease of being is in effect saying 'no' to all those things and people and places we have already said 'yes' to."

— JON KABAT-ZINN, *Coming to our Senses*

Class Three: Creating Balance

Theme

The answers are inside us all and once we learn to access them, we can share them. Sharing is the basis of conversation and making change.

Advanced Tool of Vision: Finding Balance

How do you keep what you want to keep, and change what you want to change?

Advanced Tool of Vision: Conversation

How do you balance your needs with those of others?

Vision and Balance

Let us start with your definition of balance. Use individual words or a short paragraph to describe the purpose and meaning of balance for you. Be spontaneous, write what flows easily from your heart and mind.

_____

_____

_____

_____

_____

_____

_____

Balance can be broadly defined:

• As when an object remains reasonably steady in a particular position on a narrow base. For people, this commonly involves remaining upright and steady on our feet.

• As involving the opposition of equal forces; meaning a state in which two opposing forces or factors of equal strength or importance neutralize each other so that stability is maintained. For example, our account ledgers record the balance between accounts payable and receivable.

• As achieving a state of harmony in which various parts form a satisfying and harmonious whole and nothing is out of proportion or unduly emphasized at the expense of other parts. A room's décor may balance its different components. A painting or garden balances different forms and colors.

• As a precarious position; whereby an object is placed in a position where it is or seems to be assessing something; to compare the relative importance of different factors or alternatives before making a choice or decision; for example, to balance the pros and cons of a proposal before moving ahead.

Balance is not static, but rather an adjustable concept that benefits from thoughtful tinkering. As you routinely multi-task during the day, be aware of your feelings — they guide your thoughts and help you make appropriate adjustments. For example, if you feel tired you might balance your time with a break or nap. If you feel pressure, you may slow down. If you feel cramped up indoors, take a walk outside. If you've been procrastinating, try "just doing it."

Imbalances

How do you define imbalance?

_____

_____

_____

_____

_____

Harmony and equilibrium can be disrupted when one force (within ourselves or between ourselves and others) blocks the flow needed to stabilize movement. Blockage becomes a form of domination, or emphasis of one element over another.

To illustrate this point, imagine a see-saw. When two people at either end are aligned, the see-saw easily pivots up and down. But when one person suddenly stops pushing off from the ground, the see-saw remains stationary and the other person is stuck up in the air. When the person on the ground calls,"I'm in control! I'll tell you when it's time to come down," the elevated person has no choice and the situation has become unbalanced.

Red Flags

A minor disruption, or imbalance, can be called a red flag. You can recognize a red flag by visual or somatic signs — just enough to warrant your attention. You lose your sense of ease and comfort; things start to feel overly complicated. Think of a red flag when you see or hear something that catches your eye or gets into your ear. Perhaps a friend insults you once too often or asks too many favors, or your lawyer never returns phone calls. This impression can be fleeting and therefore subtle.

A red flag is a helpful warning sign. Once identified, a red flag enables us to handle the imbalance before it progresses into a full-blown obstacle. Pay attention to what you think and feel because a red flag can be easily ignored.

Here's an example of how one couple handled red flags:

Mary and Peter loved sports: skiing in the winter, golfing in the spring, summer, and fall. Seemingly in tandem, they easily made decisions about where to go in each season. Automatic pilot had slipped into their relationship and its activities.

But Mary's enthusiasm for their common activities began to wane. It took her longer to make up her mind about where and when to travel. Packing became more and more onerous and she began to feel disorganized. Mary's procrastination and inability to make travel decisions started to frustrate Peter. They were no longer in sync as a couple, though neither had yet identified this red flag.

But over time Mary began to connect the dots between her feelings and her indecisiveness. She was taking a drawing course at the local art center and displayed enough talent to qualify for the annual art show. Feeling focused and energized by her newly recognized artistic achievement, she wanted to devote more time and energy to her art projects and her classmates, and did not want to go skiing so often.

The more enthusiastic Mary became about her art classes, the more frustrated Peter began to feel. The red flag was still unnoticed but, nonetheless changing the alignment in their relationship. The see-saw metaphor was at work, and Mary was keeping him up in the air! It was time to acknowledge and deal with the red flag in Mary's behavior before it grew into a full blown obstacle that would further threaten the integrity of their relationship. Peter initiated an honest discussion about re-thinking each of their wishes, and re-aligning their couple activities.

Obstacles

A greater imbalance may become an obstacle. Obstacles often require more effort to resolve than red flags. Sometimes obstacles reflect long-held beliefs or conflicts. Addressing some obstacles may entail counseling or professional intervention.

Think of a red flag as a door that needs some jiggling, while obstacles appear like stuck doors that can't open.

Here is a story of how one couple ignored the red flags and faced an obstacle to their balance:

For many years, Debra and Alex maintained a workable balance in their marriage: she managed the couple's social life while he managed his own work and leisure schedule. Alex was an agreeable person, with flexible work hours, who went along with whatever social commitments his wife made for them.

When Alex's priorities began to shift from his work to leisure activities, like sailing and long distance running, discontent rippled through their relationship. Suddenly Alex didn't want Debra to set his social plans. In fact, he didn't want to socialize much at all, but wanted to spend more time with just a few people on his boat. Debra was eager to get out of the house and see others. She disliked sailing so frequently and found it boring. Alex's insistence on fulfilling his personal leisure activities at the expense of their social life became a red flag in this relationship. Ultimately, their resentment of each other and increasing separateness grew into an obstacle. The couple did not seek professional help. They divorced a few years later.

Exercise One: Me, Us, and Them

We each must find a unique way to juggle our own needs with those of our partner, our family, or others around us.

Heightened awareness helps you to spot red flags and obstacles that threaten the balance of your life.

Balance requires cooperation — between you and yourself, and between yourself and others. A "Me, Us, and Them" Conversation is about clear and respectful communication with any important others, as you establish balance.

That's exactly what Nancy, a nurse who had volunteered in the Peace Corps in her twenties, understood when she retired. She told me:

"I want to continue using my skills, but this time in far-off places like Haiti. The Peace Corps sends calls to action whenever there is a need, for instance, a cholera epidemic. I want to go but I know that my aunt is part of the decision. Will she want me to go? She's 86 years old and we've lived in the same high-rise for 15 years. She depends on me for companionship and aid. We've never spoken about my possibly going elsewhere, but I guess I always let something intervene so my plans never took off. I will now include her in my plans and decisions, maybe speak about hiring someone to help her in my absence."

Initially, Nancy never had a "Me, Us, and Them" Conversation. She made assumptions that she failed to share with her aunt. Until Nancy changed, her aunt was not invited into the conversation about Nancy's true vision for her life.

Mike also learned that a "Me, Us, and Them" Conversation made a difference. His plan has worked happily for himself, his wife, and their daughter:

Mike wanted to retire and to continue working creatively with his hands, using the carpentry/building skills that he loved and honed over a lifetime. Also, in the last few years Mike started to daydream about a lifestyle that included more travel.

His vision was so clear that he could "picture" himself traveling from town to town and city to city, picking up light carpentry/handyman work to support his traveling expenses. At the same time he would meet and talk to people with different lifestyles. What he could not "see" was his wife refuting what she perceived as a radical change in their lifestyle and her sense of "where home is."

When his daughter moved overseas to invest in property, she asked her father if he would join her and supervise the renovations. What he envisioned became possible in a way he did not think of in the past. Mike would be able to use his skills in a more managerial way. He would be involved in the creative aspect of renovating existing properties but he would also be able to delegate. His wife fully embraced the vision of establishing a residence in one country, along with a flexible work schedule that allowed them to travel in Europe.

Mike would continue to do what he loved and knew how to do while mixing in the new, which was a focus on travel and a flexible work schedule. Realizing his vision became a win-win situation for Mike and his wife.

Mike's initial vision was clear: he wanted to use his carpentry skills and to travel. His wife's vision was also clear. She wanted a secure sense of home. Their daughter presented an unexpected opportunity, and Mike and his wife were each willing to take her up on it.

Your lifestyle changes will have a trickle-down effect on the lives of those around you. You will decide what needs to be communicated to family and friends alike as you make the changes.

What I'll Do for Me

First think of yourself. Imagine a lifestyle that will enrich you. Think of what you need most:

Sample answer:

I want a lifestyle with enriching activities and stimulating down-time. Practicing the piano gives me pleasure; I get lost in the music. A good book on my nightstand and an ongoing knitting project are essentials to feeling both creative and productive. A subscription to the Orpheus Chamber Music Orchestra and dinner at a relaxing café with friends is also a thrilling part of my life.

What I'll Do for Us

Think about the others with whom you share your daily life. This may be your spouse or domestic partner, your parent(s), your child(ren), your roommate, even your pet(s). The 'Us' in our lives, often those with whom we share a home and an emotional bond, will be called our 'daily partner.' A pet too is a partner in that its needs affect your life and daily decisions. If you live on your own and do not have a daily partner or any pets, please skip this exercise and proceed to What I'll Do for Them.

Changes you would like to make that your daily partner would not welcome:

Personal changes:

_____

_____

_____

Changes in the relationship:

_____

_____

_____

How might you achieve balance?

Sample answer:

Personal Change:
I would like to go back to school and finish my bachelor's degree.

Changes in the Relationship:
The classes and studying will compete for my time with our home chores and couple time. My partner may want to explore new activities for himself and, also, be willing to take on more of the household responsibilities.

How Might You Achieve Balance?
My partner will explore his hobby of making furniture that he can take out into the market place. Hiring a part-time cleaning service will ease up our household responsibilities. My willingness to cook and freeze food in bulk will balance with my partner's home-cooked meals and occasional restaurant treats.

Changes that your daily partner seems to want, but that you don't want:

Personal changes:

Changes in the relationship:

How might you achieve balance?

Sample answer:

Personal Changes:
My business partner wants to explore other entrepreneurial opportunities that require the closing of our joint venture.

Changes in the Relationship:
I feel anxious about my financial stability. I travel extensively and have a rich social life. How will I keep up with this if our business closes?

I've grown accustomed to the life that this income has made possible, but I know I can't take on the responsibilities alone. After years of hard work and friendship, I feel let down, if not betrayed, by my business partner.

How Might You Achieve Balance?

I will ask my business partner to remain in the venture for another year.

This will give me time to evaluate my needs and options. For example, we might sell the business and I might decide to retire. Or, I might find someone to buy out my partner and take on that share of the work.

Alternately, I might take the occasion to reawaken my unique, funky sense of style, my overall interest and love of fashion, along with my retail sales background. My good friend, who shares my passion and interest in starting a new business, also has the financial ability to share in the requisite seed money. Our credit rating is excellent and will qualify us for a business loan, if necessary. That way, I too can initiate a new business and become an enterpreneur. I can therefore be supportive of my current partner rather than resentful of the change.

My new lifestyle will also include a financial advisor who will help me with a realistic appraisal of my financial assets versus my expenses over the next 2-4 years. He or she will also assist with the writing of my budget. Sticking with a budget will help me feel less anxious.

Changes you both want to make:

Personal changes:

_____

_____

_____

Changes in the relationship:

_____

_____

How might you achieve balance?

Sample answer:

Personal Changes:
We are both growing weary of the responsibilities of owning two homes; actually three, if you count our country house used mostly by our children. We are in agreement to sell our home, but we disagree about choosing our next domicile(s).

My wife prefers our home in Arizona because of the climate and the opportunity for a full social life and involvement in the greater community. I prefer to be up north so that I can continue to work, either full or part-time, and remain involved with my current community activities. I am fearful of retiring but have not been able to articulate my fears clearly to my wife.

Changes in the Relationship:
These conflicts began to create stress in our relationship.

We have incrementally been spending more of the year living separately. I have, however, increased my time in Arizona to reduce the amount of time we live apart. I do enjoy swimming, riding my bike, and being able to exercise outdoors during the winter months. A mixture of work and play is appealing to me, but not hours and hours of activities such as golf and playing cards. I am a friendly person but not as social as my wife.

The stress these conflicts have created in our relationship interferes with our ability to work out a plan that truly reflects both our needs.

She remains in a hurry to sell and move on, and I continue to drag my feet to postpone the inevitable. Discussing future plans is impossible while we are at a standstill.

How Might You Achieve Balance?

Our marriage is important to us. The balance we ultimately achieved by living separately is temporary, but ok because it enables us to both sell our home and move on. We have agreed to rent an apartment in our home state, closer to where our children live but still within an easy commute for my work. We have also negotiated with our children to assume 100% of the non-financial responsibility for the country home.

We realized the need for each of us to compromise in order to reach a decision that is satisfactory, although not necessarily perfect. It affords me some breathing space to adjust to the idea of life after work, and rids each of us of the responsibility of our current home.

What I'll Do for Them

The "Them" means anyone or any group of people who influence your life regularly, but not every day. The "Them" in your life may include:
- Elderly parents
- Children and grandchildren
- Relatives who live long distance
- Co-workers
- Friends
- Neighbors
- Community or religious groups
- Social media friends

Exercise: List the "Them" in Your Life

Each of "Them" has an impact on your plans and the shape of your retirement. List these people who will matter to you, and what they may need as your life changes. Try to keep the descriptions to one word, such as: "Companionship, Support, Humor, Contact, Phone Calls," etc.

Name	What they need from you	What you need from them
1.		
2.		
3.		
4.		
5.		
6.		

Tips for the "Me" Conversation

The "Me" Conversation" is about honoring your own needs. Your strategy is to create a balance of what you do for "yourself" and "us" while you attempt to meet the often competing needs of "them." The following pointers will help you create balance in sensitive situations. Feel free to add to this list.

o Understand your own needs with compassion, and retain a sense of confidence.

o Build a support system of family, friends, and professionals.

o Begin to delegate to family members.

o Learn to say no without (or with as little as possible) guilt.

o Celebrate the "good times." This is crucial to maintaining the equilibrium of what you do for yourself and all the others.

o Keep your sense of humor.

o Keep up your spirits and avoid those folks who only offer criticism.

o Bear in mind that this juggling act has its ups and downs and occasional crashes. It is an ongoing challenge.

Tips for the "Us and Them" Conversation

The "Us" Conversation is about resolving differences with important others on a daily basis. The "Them" Conversation is about reconciling conflict that doesn't occur every day, but crops up now and then. When you speak with others, try to avoid the language of blame or accusation, no matter what you feel. If you want to have a good ongoing relationship, focus on fair and positive suggestions for change.

1.   Emphasize the positive: Start out on a good note. Talk about what you value in each other and in your life. Try to complain less, and describe more. Paint a clear picture of what you want.

2.   Use the "I" statement: We cannot control the behavior of others by reminding and nagging. We can, however, learn to effectively communicate our preferences and desires to others. Here are two examples:

"I really miss you and our time together. Let's put our heads together and plan a fun activity just for the two of us."

"Honey, I have lots of energy today so I am heading to the basement to start the spring clean up." (By the way, do not expect that your partner will follow your cue. Be prepared to begin the process on your own and check your negative feelings at the basement door.)

3.   Commit time: Making time for your partner, family, and friends is a form of non-verbal but, nonetheless, effective communication. It says that 'you are important' and 'I am here for you.' Plan activities with important others in your life.

Wrap Up Exercise: Life Balance. In 5-10 minutes write a description of the balance in your new life that you want to create between "Me, Us, and Them":

_____

_____

_____

_____

_____

_____

_____

_____

_____

_____

_____

_____

_____

Sample Life Balance description:

I realize that my new lifestyle, without definitive work hours, creates a space that I can easily fill with needs from "Us and Them." First and foremost, I need to emphasize the focus of "Me." This is challenging but doable. I may journal about it, and create a support team of two close friends whom I'll speak with twice a week. I will also schedule in special "dates with myself."

Secondly, I am an articulate person out in the world. It is time to bring these skills into my personal relationships. Practicing in front of the mirror and listening to my voice on audio will be helpful in transferring these attributes to the "Us and Them" in my life.

Knowing what I want and need is crucial! It's important to update my "What I'll Do for Me" on a regular basis.

Lisa, a workshop participant, shared her lack of a plan for a transition from a family business to the structureless world of the unemployed. "Since my retirement was forced on me I did not pay much attention to the way I would be spending it. I focused more on my husband's happiness and adjustment than my own." Lisa appeared to have confused an involuntary retirement with a life that lacks personal options. She needed to learn how to have a "Me, Us, and Them" Conversation. Certainly, there was not enough "Me" in her vocabulary.

"The workshop taught me that I needed to think of myself. What makes me tick? What can I do to make myself happy? I realized that I missed my days of volunteering. Also, I understood that my husband would need to make his own individual decisions. It was very helpful to learn that we do have a degree of control over our life experiences. Once I have experience taking care of my needs it will be easier to give to the 'Us' and 'Them' in my life."

How does it feel to identify the conflicts and balances in your life?

Was it easiest to write about What I'll do for "Me," for "Us," or for "Them?"

Does your Life Balance Description feel realistic?

Exercise Two: Implementing Balance Between Keepers and Changers —
Making It Happen

Homework Review

Consider your first Keeper and the three steps you listed on page 59. Do you notice any Red Flags or perceive Obstacles to taking your steps? What makes it all seem difficult or impossible? These perceptions of difficulty will be called Challenges. As we seek to implement Keepers and Changers in our lives, such Challenges may confound us and block movement. We may spend so much time worrying about Challenges that we do nothing else.

Tracking the Challenges

The following workbook exercises are designed to help you clarify Challenges that may impede your steps. Sometimes these impediments are real, other times they are imagined. Often, there is a viable way to overcome them.

Proposing Solutions

Once you have identified the Challenges you will then use the tools of vision you've been practicing — quick or expanded reflection — to create solutions. For example, where might you introduce balance between conflicting needs? How can you take responsibility to solve logistical problems? What "Me, Us, and Them" Conversations might you initiate?

First, we'll explore the Keepers — the positive aspects of your life that you wish to sustain and enhance.

Study the sample on the facing page. Notice that the Challenges can often be written in one sentence: "I have a wish, but here's the problem." (*I want to visit them regularly, but our budget is tight and calendar is packed.*)

The solutions can be proposed in an equally straightforward sentence. Allow them to be bold and simple. These prompts will help you identify the actions you wish to take. Make sure they're realistic, and set a date that will benchmark your doing them.

KEEPER: _Closeness with my grandchildren_

STEPS with CHALLENGES:

 I want to visit them regularly but our budget is tight and calendar is packed.

 My husband expresses discomfort about travel.

 I want to connect over Skype but I'm lousy with technology and feel foreign from it. It's a "young" thing.

STEPS with SOLUTIONS: DATE:

Will work out a calendar and budget, with my husband and financial planner.   _by New Year_

Will offer the family a yearly visit to us, so my husband doesn't have to travel.   _by son's birthday, 1/16_

My granddaughter will help me set up an account and teach me Skype on her next visit.   _when she visits, 4/10_

The Changers may be more tricky because we don't know exactly what they will feel like or how they'll happen.

The person who just wrote about closeness with her grandchildren knows what that feels like. She knows it means spending actual time together and sharing experiences. She's open to trying Skype as a way of maintaining regular contact when she's no longer living near them.

But she doesn't know how to lose 10 pounds. Perhaps she's always been a little overweight or had trouble controlling her diet and her eating patterns.

In the Changer sample on the opposite page, she admits that she doesn't know her first step. It's fine not to know! That is often a huge Challenge to doing anything: *I don't know what to do first, or where to turn.* If that is how you feel then write it.

She then looks at what's logical, what she has tried in the past that hasn't worked.

Using tools of vision, she realizes that the way through her usual pitfall is to surround herself with a knowledgeable and supportive group. If she does so, others can assist her in sustaining her diet. Facilitators and other participants in the program will help her reach her weight loss goal. She realizes that she's tried "going it alone," and that this approach has never been helpful. Her tools of vision have helped her to foresee another approach.

She's also given herself 3 weeks of "research time." She can try attending different meetings and speaking with people who've benefitted from different programs. She might find that Weight Watchers and Overeaters Anonymous are complementary, and will offer double support if she does both.

After she completes her research step she will take the step to formally begin a program. Wisely, she has given herself over 3 months in which to lose the full 10 pounds. If she does so quicker, it's all well and good.

Her final step is to lose 10 pounds by her birthday.

Can you imagine a better birthday present than a healthier body to walk around in every day?

CHANGER: _Lose 10 pounds_

STEPS WITH CHALLENGES:

 I don't even know my first step. I have no idea how to begin, who to turn to.

 It's logical to diet, but diets never work for me. I do them for 3 days and reward myself by over-eating.

STEPS WITH SOLUTIONS:

DATE:

 I will research programs like Weight Watchers or O.A. that offer a structure and group support.   _March 1_

 I will commit to a program and follow whatever diet and fitness plan they recommend.   _March 21_

 I will lose 10 pounds by my birthday.   _July 8_

Use the pages that follow to identify your Challenges — your fears, pitfalls, and apprehensions — about making these desires and changes happen in your life.

Take the opportunity to be candid with yourself.

Then use the tools of vision to formulate solutions that feel possible and exciting, even if they involve some time, work, and adjustment.

TIP Be simple, bold, and clear. Tell it like it is. Use straightforward language. Complain, if you need to.

TIP Don't stay in complaint mode. Think constructively and creatively. Find a way through the Challenges. Remember, the answers to all of your questions are inside you.

TIP Take the time to tune in and listen to yourself. Remember that *power vision* honors your dreams and makes sense for your life.

TIP Set dates that are realistic for you to achieve these goals and steps.

We'll start with a Changer ... just to shake things up a bit.

CHANGER: _____

STEPS with CHALLENGES:

⊘ _____
_____

⊘ _____
_____

⊘ _____
_____

STEPS with SOLUTIONS:

Date:

_____
_____   _____

_____
_____   _____

_____
_____   _____

KEEPER: _____

STEPS with CHALLENGES:

_____
_____

_____
_____

_____
_____

STEPS with SOLUTIONS:

DATE:

_____
_____   _____

_____
_____   _____

_____
_____   _____

CHANGER: _____

STEPS with CHALLENGES:

_____
_____

_____
_____

_____
_____

STEPS with SOLUTIONS:

Date:

_____
_____   _____

_____
_____   _____

_____
_____   _____

KEEPER: _____

STEPS with CHALLENGES:

_____
_____

_____
_____

_____
_____

STEPS with SOLUTIONS: Date:

_____
_____   _____

_____
_____   _____

_____
_____   _____

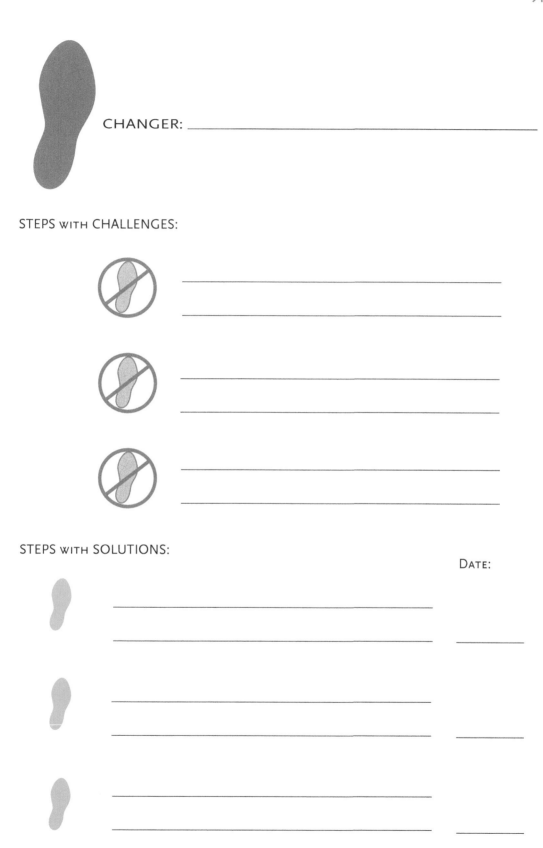

CHANGER: _____

STEPS with CHALLENGES:

_____
_____

_____
_____

_____
_____

STEPS with SOLUTIONS:

Date:

_____

_____   _____

_____

_____   _____

_____

_____   _____

KEEPER: _____

STEPS with CHALLENGES:

_____
_____

_____
_____

_____
_____

STEPS with SOLUTIONS:

DATE:

_____
_____   _____

_____
_____   _____

_____
_____   _____

CHANGER: _____

STEPS with CHALLENGES:

_____
_____

_____
_____

_____
_____

STEPS with SOLUTIONS:

Date:

_____
_____ _____

_____
_____ _____

_____
_____ _____

KEEPER: _____

STEPS with CHALLENGES:

_____

_____

_____

_____

_____

_____

STEPS with SOLUTIONS: DATE:

_____

_____   _____

_____

_____   _____

_____

_____   _____

Congratulations!

This exercise takes a lot of focus and honesty.
In writing down your plans, you have taken a huge step in your journey.

Establishing, losing, and re-creating balance is a life-time pursuit.

Relationships require a certain amount of resiliency to ride the waves when the surf grows stronger and more unpredictable.

Your Keepers and Changers are the signposts on your roadmap. They help you to navigate your travels, and they keep you anchored. Make a schedule so that you remember to re-visit them and make any necessary changes as you keep moving. There are more Keepers and Changers pages at the end of the book that you can use after the class is complete.

Exercise Three: Balancing New Identity with the Old

Peeling the Artichoke

Look at the answers that came to you as you meditated on your sense of purpose on page 61. Take a moment now to describe your sense of purpose: Is it expressed in your current life?

_____

_____

_____

_____

_____

At times, in order to express our sense of purpose we must let go of something that has felt safe. You experienced doing that in the homework exercise on page 62 where you did one thing differently. You learned how it felt to even make one minor adjustment in your routine. What did that teach you?

_____

_____

The process of letting go as transitions demand is an uneven journey. You will experience one step forward and two steps backward. But always remember that while ambivalence is an annoying travel companion, you are the navigator and perseverance is the engine.

The main thing to remember is this: If you are ever to become the person you want to be, use the things you know how to do and enjoy as a basis for your retirement life.

On the outside, you may need to get rid of the values and identity that sustained you during the first half of your life in order to get in touch with the person on the inside. You'll need to "Peel the Artichoke," or find out who you are, rather than who your job and society say you are.

Katherine, a workshop participant, started to "Peel the Artichoke." She did so in order to search for an identity outside of her profession. First she imagined herself at a social gathering after retirement. The outcome demonstrated her singular identity as a teacher. She had no words to describe who she was to be in her post-retirement years and realized that her image of a traditional leisure retirement would result in a very quiet life. As a single woman, her friendships and interests revolved mainly around work and its related activities. She recognized that she needed a plan to create a life that included what she loved to do, along with the camaraderie of friends.

Her "peeling" process uncovered an interest in tennis. She had played the game sporadically over the years. Retirement would give her the luxury of time since tennis requires practice as well as several hours to play. At the same time she could expand her social circle by joining a local club.

Katherine was lucky that her retirement was a few years down the road. Her first step was to start taking tennis lessons and practice regularly. She would improve her game and discover whether she truly loved playing this sport on a regular basis. She would also be able to keep her eyes open for a companion with whom to share her new social activities. Katherine had just begun her "peeling" process.

You Can Get Some Satisfaction

We Peel the Artichoke to find what gives us the most satisfaction.

Satisfaction is defined as "anything that brings pleasure or contentment." And while everyone experiences ups and downs, those things that bring you satisfaction help to define who you are as much as the challenges do.

Think of the satisfying things in your life as part of your autobiography. Then think about re-writing it to incorporate the satisfactions of the future life you imagine.

The following exercise will help the process of "peeling" in order to reach the core of who you want to be. The answers are essential components in your road-map as you transition from the familiar to the new in your quest for a creative retirement.

Decide what to bring into your next phase by seeing what is important and what isn't. You can leave behind what is no longer important. Describe how each of these aspects of your former job has affected your life. Then prioritize each satisfaction from one to four, with one being the most important and four the least.

Colleague collaboration:
> *the stimulation of exchanging ideas and feedback in an*
> *energized environment*

Challenge and Opportunity:
> *making a unique contribution to the company's goals*

The Good Times:
> *parties and other fun events*

Status:
> *enjoying how others perceive your level in the hierarchy*

You Are What You Do

The following exercise will start your own "peeling" process.

1. Along with other satisfactions, employment provides an identity. How much do you depend upon what you do for the recognition and respect you enjoy? Spell it out.

_____

_____

2. You are retired and attend a social event. You introduce yourself to your fellow guests. What do you say to identify yourself?

_____

_____

_____

_____

_____

_____

_____

If you wish, make a drawing or paste an image that represents your "Peeled Artichoke" in the space below:

Homework Assignments

1: Complete listing as many Keepers and Changers steps as you can, on pages 87-94. Include a "Me, Us, and Them Conversation" if one is needed for your Solution Steps.

2: Take 5-10 minutes, using the lens of "Balance," to write a short narrative about how you might create balance between Work and Play in your new life. The challenge that achieving this balance presents for you is obviously influenced by your prior work and play experiences. Would you consider yourself as having been addicted to either work or play? Or, did you transition smoothly between these two parts of your life?

3: Remember a dream and write it down in as much detail as possible.

TIP Record your dream, or whatever you can remember, upon awakening, whether in the middle of the night or as your first activity in the morning. Feel free to add interpretations. Full sentences are not required; just a word, idea, or image is all you need. Do not dismiss any thoughts or feelings. Remember: What you think and feel is important. Go to your "date place" to contemplate the dream.

"Making your creative dreams real requires you to be involved, inspired, and forward-moving even when you feel none of these things. Especially when you feel blocked, lost, and crabby and like hiding most of all."

— SARK (*Susan Ariel Rainbow Kennedy*)

Making Your Creative Dreams Real

Class Four: Living the Dream

Theme:

The answers are inside us all and once we learn to access them, we can share them. Sharing is the basis of conversation. Sharing means expressing ourselves with trust, listening to others with respect, and creating something new with vision.

Advanced Tool of Vision:

Dreams and Daydreams

What Does it Mean to Be a Person of Vision?

Person of Vision is a term coined for this workbook. It speaks of the person who has toured him or herself with a sightseer's eye and learned what to keep and what to change. This person fluently uses the tools of vision we've introduced. He or she walks through life with a high degree of awareness of self, in touch with inner answers that become the basis of an ongoing vision. He or she takes the steps necessary to navigate life's demands and transitions, rather than merely react to them.

Vision was discussed at the beginning of this workshop. Remember these pointers:

• Visions can come to you as a word, a sentence, a paragraph, or an image — or, as we'll see, in a dream or daydream. Whatever it is, a vision reflects you and what you want for your life.

• As you update your plans over the years, continue to create a record of your visions by putting words in a journal and/or pasting the pictures in a scrapbook.

• Treat yourself to the time you need to connect with your visions.

There's a difference between having a life and designing a life. The person of vision designs his or her life.

This person is you!

Homework Review

You completed your Keepers and Changers Steps. What happened? Any surprises? Any red flags raised? Any tweaking needed? What did you learn about yourself or anyone else in your life?

_____

_____

_____

_____

Wrap up for Keepers and Changers ~ a final look over

You've spent these past weeks reviewing your life, identifying Keepers and Changers, and listing the challenges and specific steps they entail. With all this in mind, write a short narrative about how these different Keepers and Changers will shape your new life:

How my Keepers will shape my new life:

_____

_____

_____

_____

How my Changers will shape my new life:

_____

_____

_____

_____

Dream Work: Exploring dreams through different lenses

Night dreams, since they are uncensored, are great tools of Vision.

The dreams you experience while asleep are important. They remind you of what you want to accomplish in your life. Unfortunately, many people view dreams as the brain's way of letting off steam or replaying events or wishful thinking. These opinions are traps that prevent you from listening to, and using, your dreams. Don't allow yourself to fall into the trap of believing that your night dreams don't matter. Here are ways to counteract any dream resistance you might have.

Trap	Tip
Dreams are only about immediate nonsense.	Dreams portray what you want. They have themes. Pay attention to them.
Dreams are illogical.	Unscramble dream fragments and reassemble them like parts of a puzzle.
Dreams are personal.	Share them. You may be happily surprised by others' interpretations.
Dreams are foolish.	Trust your instincts. You are your own best expert.
Dreams aren't part of the real world.	Dreams are you, uncensored. They offer a perspective that is unique to you.
Dreams are fleeting.	Dreams are ephemeral, but telling.

Homework Review:

The exercises in this book are intended to strengthen your Power Vision and raise your awareness of what you truly want. Look at the dream you described on page 101 and answer whatever you can in the questions below.

What feelings arise when you think back to the dream? Are they feelings that you welcome or that you censor in your waking life?

Using the "Keepers and Changers" lens, what do you see in the dream from the present or from the past that you'd like to keep or reawaken in your life?

What in the dream speaks out to you about change in your life?

Night Dreams and Daydreams

Daydreams are another route you can take to access what has been censored. Easier to understand than night dreams, daydreams are a little story that you tell yourself. Do you ever find yourself distracted? At those moments, what do you think about?

_____

_____

_____

Write any of your recent daydreams.

_____

_____

_____

Do they overlap or contrast with your night dream?

_____

_____

_____

What might they may be saying?

_____

_____

_____

_____

WRAP UP Continue to pay careful attention to all your dreams. We have learned that they help you to define your quests and motivate you to form a vision of what you want to accomplish.

Homework Review:

Balance between Work and Play

Reveiw what you have written on page 100 about balancing work and play in your life. Is there any connection between this vision of balance and what you see in your daydreams? If you see a connection, please describe it.

Aligning Your Vision to Your Sense of Purpose

Consider your Sense of Purpose from the exercise on page 61. The following three exercises will help you identify how your sense of purpose harmonizes with your Keeper and Changers and guiding Vision of retirement.

FIRST VISION: Be spontaneous, off-the-top-of-your-head. In the space below, list 4 key words — such as *connected, peaceful, artistic, exciting* — to describe your Sense of Purpose in your Vision for retirement.

1. _____

2. _____

3. _____

4. _____

SECOND VISION: Write a sentence for each key word to further clarify how your Sense of Purpose informs your Vision for your retirement such as: *I will sustain my wonderful friendships and connections* or *With more time, I will be productive artistically*.

1. _____

2. _____

3. _____

4. _____

THIRD VISION: Suppose you're 85. It's your birthday and you are looking back at your life. You are in good physical and mental health. Where do you live? How do you spend your days? Who surrounds you? Check to see that these answers harmonize with your Sense of Purpose.

_____

_____

_____

_____

_____

_____

_____

Legacy: Envisioning a Future Based on Your Dreams

Legacy is something of value that you leave for the benefit of others. Remember that a legacy can be financial, intellectual, emotional, or spiritual. Whatever form it takes, it requires some planning and belongs in the retirement conversation.

What do you want your legacy to your family to be?

What do you want your legacy to your friends to be?

What do you want your legacy to your community to be?

Wrap Up of the Journey: Create Your Mission Statement

At the end of Section Two on page 57 you began a "Business Plan" for your retirement. You thought of yourself as an entrepreneur and envisioned your life, in retirement, as a start-up company that you are creating. You gave this company a name, an aim, and a success team. Throughout this workbook, you've refined your plan and become more specific about what it will include.

Part I – A Different Way of Seeing crystallized your vision, and gave voice to your possibilities for changes and adaptations. "Light bulb" moments were hatched and visions were clarified!

Part II – A Different Way of Being cleared the path so you could connect with your personal epiphany. You learned the nuts and bolts of building the psychological space and personal awareness required to launch dreams into a new life; you learned to create steps and conquer resistance so your Vision, goals, and action plan can materialize.

You learned to expand and refresh your worldview, to answer the door when change and opportunity knocks — or to choose freely to turn it down and even lock the door.

You learned from your role models and created a personal inventory of who you are and who you want to be.

You figured out what to keep and what to change as you created the right balance between "Me, Us, and Them." The exercises coached you to increase your tolerance for change by encouraging you to do at least one thing differently.

You created a new psychological path by mentally and physically de-cluttering your life. That, in turn cleared the way for your vision, goals, and action plan to materialize.

You "Peeled the Artichoke" in search of the person you want to be that exists underneath the layers of your current life. You learned how to look at yourself objectively once the structure of work changes. You learned to look at your dreams and daydreams for further insight. You practiced communicating your needs and desires to the world around you in conversation.

You were shown how to launch your retirement, or whatever lifestyle change you desire, exactly the same way you would begin any new enterprise — that is, proactively. You now understand Vision and how to use it as a tool to enrich your life. You came away with a list of practical and manageable steps.

Taking all this into account, you will now write your Mission Statement for the start-up company you envision as your retirement.

Here are some steps and tips that will help you write a Mission Statement for your "start-up."

1. Remember that the business plan you develop for your embryonic company named Retirement is the blueprint for its operation and success.
2. Imagine your business plan will be comprised of the workbook exercise outcomes. As you take your journey, and travel the twists and turns of this process, these materials will be refined, modified, and ultimately chosen to become your company.
3. Start your business plan with your vision of who you are and what you want your life to be in retirement.
4. Break the plan into individual steps. Be open to brain-storming with other people.
5. Look at the long-term goals, down the road, and break them into shorter goals, to begin your work. Apply a time line so that your goals are measurable.
6. Implementing your goals becomes your action plan.

Exercise: Write the Mission Statement

Take 10 minutes to describe your company's purpose in one paragraph that will serve as your Mission Statement. You may write it in first person (an "I" voice) or in third person (a "he" or "she" voice), whichever way you feel more comfortable. (*For sample answers, see page 114.*)

Company Name:

Mission Statement:

Two sample Company Mission Statements:

A Frugal Feast

A Frugal Feast will take off when I retire in June. After that, I will work with my financial advisor to plan a monthly budget to sponsor my joyfully, happily, finally FREE time. No more office, no more desk, no more boss breathing down my neck. No more salary too … and not much by way of savings. But between Social Security and what's left of my 401 K, I'll have enough for rent, food, and prescription drugs. I can walk in the park, read, rent movies on Netflix, get on Facebook, and meet old friends for coffee. I will enjoy my freedom each day and make the most of my small nest egg.

Cora in Florida

Cora In Florida brings an accomplished oil painter to the land of palm trees and flora that she has craved for decades. Cora In Florida will launch once Cora sells her home in Happague, NY and moves to Miami Beach permanently. She will work out a plan with her stock broker to supplement her sales of art work with investment dividends. Beside her in this journey will be Graham, her beau of 4 years, numerous friends from Florida and New York, and the collectors who love her paintings.

Wrap Up of the Journey: Create Your Timeline

In the last exercise of this book, you will create an action plan that will propel your dreams into the life that you imagine or, better, to the life that you have not entirely imagined. That new life can become your day-to-day reality.

The Sample Timeline on the next page will demonstrate how to use your Keepers and Changers steps to help track and concretize your wishes. Work with it as long as you need, in the following way:

1. Review your Keepers and Changers from pages 44-60.

2. Choose a Final Completion Date and pencil it in the blue box in the Timeline. You might want to choose a significant date such as New Years, your birthday, or any other time that signifies a deadline or change for you.

3. In the space provided on the Timeline, list all of your Keepers and Changers. Include the completion dates you wrote for each of them on pages 87-94. Write in pencil so that dates can be easily changed.

4. Check off each Keeper and Changer as you complete each action step.

5. Once you complete the first Timeline, try doing another one next year with the workbook sheets provided on pages 118-126.

Do not be surprised or discouraged if dates must be changed. Be generous with yourself in granting extensions. Just cross out or erase one date and write another. It is better to keep going than to scold yourself for not having gotten there. Remember: if you find yourself struggling, congratulate yourself: you're on the right road.

FINAL TIP The journey toward becoming a Person of Vision prompts conversation — first with yourself, and then with others. Retirement can function as the refinement of dreams and goals you desire for your life.

Anything is possible.

T I M E L I N E
for Creating a New Life

Keeper:

Optimism

Keeper:

Date:
September 1

Friendship with Anne

Date:
June 10

Keeper:

Interest in art

Date:
June 10

Keeper:

Closeness with
grandchildren

Date:
April 10

Changer:

Study Spanish

Date:
September 1

Changer:

More communication with Bob

Date:
September 1

Changer:

Lose 5 more pounds

Date:
September 1

Changer:

Lose 10 pounds

Date:
July 8

Final Completion Date:

September 1

NOTES:

Weight Watchers and OA both good for different reasons.
Anne's new phone number: 387-980-5623
Spanish tutor: Magdalena 889-956-3397

T I M E L I N E
for Creating a New Life

Keeper:

_____

Date:

_____

Keeper:

_____

Date:

_____

Keeper:

_____

Date:

_____

Keeper:

_____

Date:

_____

Changer:

_____

Date:

_____

Changer:

_____

Date:

_____

Changer:

_____

Date:

_____

Changer:

_____

Date:

_____

Final Completion Date:

_____

NOTES:

_____

_____

_____

_____

KEEPER: _____

STEPS WITH CHALLENGES:

_____

_____

_____

_____

_____

_____

STEPS WITH SOLUTIONS: DATE:

_____

_____   _____

_____

_____   _____

_____

_____   _____

CHANGER: _____

STEPS with CHALLENGES:

_____
_____

_____
_____

_____
_____

STEPS with SOLUTIONS:

DATE:

_____
_____   _____

_____
_____   _____

_____
_____   _____

KEEPER: _____

STEPS with CHALLENGES:

_____

_____

_____

_____

_____

_____

STEPS with SOLUTIONS: Date:

_____

_____   _____

_____

_____   _____

_____

_____   _____

CHANGER: _____

STEPS with CHALLENGES:

🚫 _____
_____

🚫 _____
_____

🚫 _____
_____

STEPS with SOLUTIONS:

Date:

_____
_____   _____

_____
_____   _____

_____
_____   _____

KEEPER: _____

STEPS with CHALLENGES:

_____
_____

_____
_____

_____
_____

STEPS with SOLUTIONS: Date:

_____   _____

_____   _____

_____   _____

CHANGER: _____

STEPS with CHALLENGES:

_____
_____

_____
_____

_____
_____

STEPS with SOLUTIONS:

DATE:

_____
_____   _____

_____
_____   _____

_____
_____   _____

KEEPER: _____

STEPS with CHALLENGES:

_____
_____

_____
_____

_____
_____

STEPS with SOLUTIONS: DATE:

_____
_____   _____

_____
_____   _____

_____
_____   _____

CHANGER: _____

STEPS with CHALLENGES:

_____
_____

_____
_____

_____
_____

STEPS with SOLUTIONS:

_____
_____ _____

_____
_____ _____

_____
_____ _____

T I M E L I N E
for Creating a New Life

Keeper:

_____

Date:

_____

Keeper:

_____

Date:

_____

Keeper:

_____

Date:

_____

Keeper:

_____

Date:

_____

Changer:

_____

Date:

_____

Changer:

_____

Date:

_____

Changer:

_____

Date:

_____

Changer:

_____

Date:

_____

Final Completion Date:

_____

NOTES:

_____

_____

_____

_____

About the Author

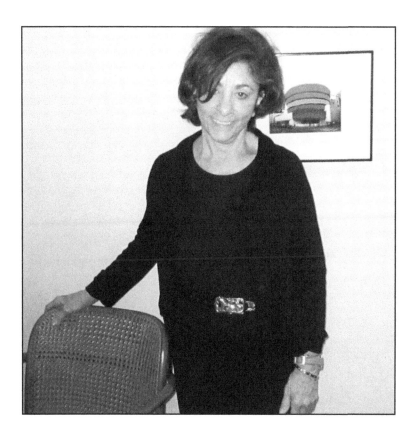

Phyllis R. Weingarten, ACSW LCSW is a licensed clinical social worker whose career spanned public and private practices. Her background and experiences influenced her own retirement, and inspired her workshop *When Every Day Is Saturday*. The workshop was then expanded into this workbook.

Phyllis earned her MSSW from the Columbia University School of Social Work and an Advanced Certificate in Clinical Social Work from New York University. She lives with her husband in New York City and Palm Beach Gardens, Florida.

CPSIA information can be obtained at www.ICGtesting.com
Printed in the USA
LVOW02s0222221214

419898LV00009B/992/P

9 780615 862767